BACK TO THE FUTURE OF MARKETING

PRovolve* or Perish

GEORGIOS KOTSOLIOS

PARTRIDGE
A Penguin Random House Company

* *Proactively evolve on a professional level*

To order additional copies of this book, contact
Toll Free 800 101 2657 (Singapore)
Toll Free 1 800 81 7340 (Malaysia)
orders.singapore@partridgepublishing.com

www.partridgepublishing.com/singapore

Follow the author's blog DubaiGreek and connect with him through:

Twitter: @Georgekotsolios

Hotmail: geokotsolios@hotmail.com

To my adoring parents for making me who I am

To my loving wife for always encouraging
me to reach my full potential

To my darling daughter *for ever*

Epigraph

"*I tell the players that the bus is moving. The club has to progress and the bus wouldn't wait for them. I tell them to get on board.*"

Sir Alex Fergusson

Preface

By the mere virtue of my current position as Head of PR at one of Dubai's biggest retailer and trading houses, I sit at the core of a portfolio of retail brands from every sector; furniture to fashion, cars to toys, consumer electronics to speedboats, watches and jewellery. As I got myself more involved into the different businesses, one trend started cropping up, time and time again; technological advances at different stages throughout the supply chain, from the manufacturing of the product, to shipping to the local market, to marketing and the final sales and after sales phase, mean that businesses need to innovate and renovate the way they interact with their customers.

This book blends this trend with lots of desk top research about changing consumer habits and technology, my passion for football and a very vivid imagination as to the shape of things to come. My long experience in PR and marketing intertwines with facts and fiction about a host of different things to concoct a medley of business and fiction, a genre still waiting to be discovered.

Chapter One

If I were the coach of Team Marketing in charge of our participation at the 2010 FIFA World Cup, here is how my first choice of players would look like:

1. **PR—Goalkeeper:** The most important position for any team with an ambition to keep a clean sheet. Avoiding defeat should always be the top priority for the coach of Team Marketing and a good goalie would go a long way to protect the reputation of his team and the coach's credentials. To win you must concede less than you score and as is the case 'PR offers more for less'.

2. **Digital—Right Back:** He is fit, flexible and focused in going the extra mile, however the coach of Team Marketing still doesn't know how to extract optimal value out of him. As an advocate of the adage that a good offense is a strong defence the coach prefers to keep one of his star players at the back till he decides what to do with him.

3. **Promotion—Left Back:** He has been around for a while but seems to have lost a bit of his lustre, looks tired and out of ideas. Needs to find his lost mojo and fitness otherwise his position in the starting line-up is at stake. He reacts well to the manager's instructions but fails to take any initiative during the match.

4. **Research—Centre Back:** He asks a lot of questions to anyone near him as he uses his inquisitive skills to analyse the strengths

of the opponent before he tackles any challenge thrown at him. He is one of the most useful members of the team and has the ability to rise above his defensive duties when required.

5. **Media Planning—Sweeper**: He is calm and full of confidence, he can see the whole game from a position of strength when his team is attacking and his perspective helps him set the tone and orchestrate his team mates' movements on the pitch.

6. **Branding—Central Midfielder**: With a blank canvas to cover, he does a lot of planning which rarely manifests itself, but its laborious approach and hard work is an essential backbone ingredient at the hands of a good Marketing coach who advocates the 4-3-3 formation.

7. **Social—Right Wing:** He is the Ronaldo of Team Marketing. He is young, fast-paced, sexy, with a versatile repertoire and millions of followers worldwide; he is also incredibly arrogant believing that he is the best of the rest of his team mates and a tad immature especially when the connection is slow.

8. **Events—Midfielder:** He is glamorous and eccentric, a heart throb and a favourite with the female fans but his performance is totally dependent on his pay check. On his good day he lifts the spirits of the whole team causing headaches to the opponents. On his bad day, his only contribution is a nasty day-after hangover.

9. **Media Buying—Centre Forward**: He is the team's striker, its most prolific scorer, when he sees an opportunity he takes it and he never misses a chance which would advance the interests of his team. In short, he is a must-have for any team who can afford him as players of his calibre are notoriously expensive.

10. **Creative—Playmaker**: He is the flashy, full of flair playmaker, enormously talented and great to watch for his gift to excite the crowds who applaud most of his moves. Irrespective of his performance on the night of the game, he commands respect and the manager is always convinced that he deserves a place in the starting line-up.

11. **Direct Marketing—Left Wing**: Working tirelessly through the line his advances are easily defended making him the least effective of the manager's attacking staff. Usually out of ideas from early on in any campaign, he tries hard to impress but the little value he brings to the team mostly goes unnoticed. He is usually the first to come off when the coach decides it's time to adjust tactics.

As the FIFA 2014 Brazil World Cup was approaching, I took a good long look at my 2010 resources, my first 11, and pondered on the team's potential in the face of the changing circumstances dictating how the modern game is now played compared to the previous tournament.

What were these new circumstances?

Well, for starters, today's sophisticated online content monitoring systems capture and decipher in seconds ions of real time chatter across Facebook, Twitter and other social media platforms. Brands analyse this chatter to deduce conclusions pertaining to perceptions people around the world have of them and their products. Technology has transformed chatter into something that can have potentially incalculable value; Consumer Insights which come directly from consumers' mouths or, to be more precise, straight from their social media accounts. Uncensored and un-vetted, impulsive and emotional 'Likes' and 'Dislikes' of the very people marketers vie to attract. Pure gold!

Possession of such insightful information is manna from heaven for the marketing community giving its privileged members a power that knows no boundaries, has no restrictions or limits as to the type of information, messaging and content they can put directly in front of their target audiences.

Companies the world over have jumped on the social media bandwagon to develop integrated campaigns that appeal to the billions of social media users. Brands have become more globally relevant than ever before as they can now talk directly and in real time to almost everyone on this planet who'd lend an eager ear to listen or rather anyone with an Internet connection and the right hash tag.

PR, digital and other communication specialists have also become a lot more social media savvy and should now work together and in unison more than ever before to provide clients holistic integrated communications solutions to satisfy the yearn for social.

This is not only important as an enabler to produce results-driven campaigns that are strategically solid and effective but it is a matter of survival in the fast-changing communications industry. Social media sits right at the middle but instead of dividing opinions as to who is its rightful owner it can serve as a catalyst for authentic integration between the disparate marketing disciplines to the benefit of agencies, clients and consumers.

In the pre-social media world, there was only so much one could do as a marketer, an advertiser and a PR man to bring a product to the attention of the masses. It would either be through a TVC, an outdoor or print advertisement, a press release, a promotional campaign at high footfall areas, an invitation-only event, a celebrity brand ambassador or at the shelf of the supermarket or store the product was on sale at. Consumer feedback was non-existent, at least in real time. There was no real conversation between products and consumers, just a one-way monologue.

Social media has changed all that for good and for the better and has unlocked the full potential of communications leaving it up to the industry itself to develop a disciplined path to actual integration.

So my team had to step up its game. Looking at my line-up of players, it was a wake-up call. To my horror I realised that a key component to my team was missing and I could no longer aspire to compete at that level in the absence of a new type of player. A game changer! But does he exist? And if so who is he and where could I find him? Should I perhaps write a Job Description to express what I am looking for, send it to footballing agents and see whether he exists? That could take too long. So I made him up instead! But I had to find a good name for him that would be descriptive of his skills and aptitudes.

Words mean things. Each word evokes a certain reaction or emotion because it is the most descriptive and direct form of human expression. Be it verbal or written, Greek or Chinese, words are highly effective communication tools. Without words, the human race and our civilization would not have evolved through the centuries. There are more words today than ever before in history and there will be more words tomorrow than there are today.

PRANDING

He is my new star player. His name is derived from three different words: Public Relations Branding and Advertising.

Pranding does exactly what the three disciplines can do together, only better, by reversing the traditional sequence of campaign origination; by having the end in mind it works backwards to achieve the specifically planned output.

Life Before Pranding was something like this:

Company X briefs advertising agency Y for the launch of a new product. Y develops campaign, presents to X for sign off. Y's objective is to create a campaign that sells the product regardless of any likely implications to the product's brand equity or reputation.

Once campaign is signed off, Y will brief branding agency Z and PR agency Omega to support the campaign. Z and Omega discover many, some or few issues with the campaign likely to cause brand image or reputational risks.

That's because branding (influential at the POS) and PR (influential in shaping consumer's emotional response to a product), did not participate or input during the campaign's development process.

Even today, before Pranding becomes an established concept, the PR agency which works closely with the Corporate Communications department is already much more attuned to a more holistic picture of what is going on within X as it enjoys a 360 view of the entire operation.

It is actively involved in content creation for the financial reviews and quarterly results media material, it is privy to confidential and public sales targets and marketing strategy, it has also probably helped formulate content about X's values, mission and corporate principles, is working on X's CSR strategy, has helped put out a fire or two on operational level (crisis management) and has contributed in and attended numerous occasions where the CEO of X shared in public or during on-on-one media interviews his views or speech on certain industry issues with an impact on the company. And due to its contribution to internal communications, Omega understands HR and staff issues better than any other external supplier. Who would argue with that?

On the other hand, the branding agency is very hands on X's various branding requirements, from letterheads to the newest web site design and from packaging of products to PoS representation.

But have they ever heard the CEO talk? Do they know how the media perceived the latest corporate announcement? Do they even care to know? More or less the same could also be said for the advertising service team. Wrong?

Here is how the roles within the team have evolved as the 2022 World Cup in Qatar is fast approaching. Let's call this period AP, After Pranding.

Omega receives client's initial brief and plots the campaign's holistic narrative having the end in mind. The end in mind is how the product is likely to be perceived by the consumer through its portrayal in earned and social media. If perceptions created at that level are negative, consumer mind sets will be resistant to any form of paid-for advertisement. Advertisers are not equipped or inclined to weigh in their campaigns the intangible cost of reputational backlash or lack of branding values and overall identity alignment between the master brand and the product in question.

In the age of Pranding, PR takes the lead by plotting the desirable happy ending to the story, then unravels Ariadne's thread towards the drawing board for the planning stages of the campaign.

If an attempt at reinventing the marketing communications wheel doesn't warrant the creation of a new word, then I don't know what is.

So off I went to the transfer window to buy Pranding, the hottest footballer alive. A truly all-rounder prodigy playmaker combining the diverse skill sets of Ronaldo and Messi into one super player made to win.

I am now confident that Team Marketing will have a great World Cup in Brazil, and with a fit Pranding we can go all the way. However, whether he would be enough to help us consistently outclass our opponents in the future world cups, it's everyone's guess.

If you were to ask me though, I would make the case that the best player of the future will have to provolve together with the constantly changing circumstances, therefore it is not long before Pranding hangs his boots. His replacement may startle everyone, for he may not even have played for a Marketing Discipline team before, a total outsider with clinical finishing skills. But before I unveil my future star-studded squad and key star signings, we still have some reading to do.

Chapter Two

To see into the future one must delve into the past and be cognizant of the present to extract and digest useful insights, trends and consumer behaviours set against backdrops that are familiar to us. And in order to be successful in any predictions, or at least as close as possible, one needs to be an expert in the subject of the journey of clairvoyance.

Back to the Future, an 80's blockbuster starring Michael J Fox as teenager Marty McFly, certainly wasn't as spot on about its take on the future; for when the character leaped three decades ahead in time he was driving on a flying car in a Futurama type of a city. The movie prompted then President Ronald Reagan, a fan of the film, to reference the movie in his 1986 State of the Union Address when he said, "Never has there been a more exciting time to be alive, a time of rousing wonder and heroic achievement. As they said in the film *Back to the Future*, 'Where we're going, we don't need roads."

This can only mean one thing; that when even Spielberg can't get it right, or to be more specific, if the script's writers Robert Zemeckis, and Bob Gale got it so terribly wrong despite having a budget of millions and a Presidential endorsement, then I could have a go at predicting what the future has in store for an industry that I have served in the last 20 years; and I would still feel good if my oracles do no justice to my posterity, albeit having very little to show for it compared to Zemeckis and his namesake and co-script writer.

And since no one can actually predict what lies ahead, only the historian of the future can prove me wrong so till then, I will remain immune to any sinister critics and critiques from gurus of the industry of marketing or the industry of film and the genre of science fiction in particular.

So let me demonstrate my Pythian prowess by making the following statement: **In the future products will** talk **directly to consumers** and I don't mean that in the metaphorical sense of the word. Cookies, detergents, packs of crisps and cereal, apparel, toys, cars, soda cans, tablet computers and smart phones, drugs, cigarettes, gum, you name it! They will all talk! And they will be multi lingual of course; in fact each product will speak nearly every language spoken anywhere in the world. Nonsense you're saying? Well, let's unravel the thread which led us here first before we reach any hastened conclusions.

It is 1992—just 22 years ago assuming you are reading this in 2014. I have just graduated from College in London and made it into my first real job as a sports journalist for a Fleet Street-based newspaper. Yes, back then most of the UK's national newspapers had their offices at this street. To be more precise, my office was in a building off Fleet Street, on inconspicuous New Fetter Lane. I had been hired as a full time writer and researcher on the back of a successful internship period by Peter Barrington, the paper's sports editor, who seemingly had appreciated my passion for sport journalism and knowledge of certain European sports which were rather underrepresented if not totally lacking from the editorial content and which was a niche many of the publication's readers craved for. For a weekly newspaper during the BI era (before Internet), we could not claim that we would break news the same way that the newswires or broadcast media could, but we would follow a rather analytical approach to add insights and viewpoints to our stories. So my job entailed quite a lot of research to obtain background information that would help me and other feature desk writers morph out our stories. So every time my editor wanted to get background information on an athlete, a team or any sporting subject that would be in focus any given week, he'd ask me to get it for him. Sounds simple? Not BI. Not exactly!

Apart from the nuance that I first had to get off my chair and take a five minute walk, up a few stairs and down a few more to get to the archive section of the paper—intimately referred between staffers as *the dungeon*—, I had to fill in long hand a request form containing the relevant keywords which I had to then pass on to Rodger, an elderly archive-keeper—for lack of a better word—who would lower his reading glasses upon my form, clear his throat a couple of times and then gather his composure, take a deep breath and help himself off his chair to drag his feet at the back of the library-like room, where a lengthy search would commence amongst shelves and files containing newspaper clippings pasted with UHU stick in A4 papers.

In the meantime and until Rodger was still looking for the appropriate files, I was just standing there, a 22-year-old, clueless and bored, eyes vacant, yet hopeful, that at some point during the same day, I would be able to return back to my desk, to triumphantly and full of pride announce to my editor that I had stricken gold, that I had managed, despite all the odds, obstacles and Rodger's nonchalance, to return with the Holy Grail, the source of all knowledge about the subject he had asked me for.

Most times I did get back holding a bruised carton folder, with the signs of ageing spreading along both covers and all four chipped, wrinkling corners. The folder would in most cases contain a few yellowing clips of my newspaper and of a few others which had reported on the subject of my search. That was it—the source of all background knowledge available to the editorial team, contained in a few poorly-maintained newspaper clips. In most cases the subject in question had been highlighted with a bright yellow marker and it was easy to identify. That would be the equivalent of today's Quick Search option in Google, I guess.

As my trips to Rodger's realm gradually became more frequent, my visitations seemed to make him tick having on him an effect similar to the one modern energy drinks have on teenagers or caffeine on our memory as per the findings of a recent study. He had become more welcoming, even mumbling "Hello" sometimes through his swollen, cracked lips bearing a permanent bleeding bump right in the middle of the lower flap. I dare say that he even looked forward to seeing me in order to get his daily opportunity to get off his chair and venture to the sea of shelves behind him into an adventure that kept his instincts and reflexes alive.

One day, as I was standing there, waiting for Rodger to return with the day's data dose, I sort of had a panic attack. "What if Rodger falls sick tomorrow? I asked myself. "What if he takes his annual leave and goes for two weeks? Who would be replacing him? How would I be able to get my hands on the information required to garnish the newspaper's stories with the detail and the background needed for our readers to get the full picture? Or, even worst, what if Rodger kicked the bucket? What then? I couldn't even bear the thought, not because I had suddenly developed a friendly disposition towards my ancient colleague from the archives department but mostly because of the panic I felt at the thought of having no access to information.

Fast forward to the second decade of the 21st century, the decade of Big Data! Some refer to it as Data Deluge. Call it what you may, it is here. And it is the delayed answer to my prayers and panacea to my fears, that despite Rodger's eventual demise from the face of this earth, human ingenuity has come up to the rescue with the right answer to my problem.

Obviously, what we are witnessing today is the result of the advent of the Internet in the ensuing two decades between the days of my daily visits to the archive section and my job today. But 22 years ago, I would be dumbfounded, if my panic attack over Rodger's potential absence from his desk had been followed by an epiphany revealing a replacement as effective and as astounding as Internet search engines.

The world's technological per-capita capacity to store information has roughly doubled every 40 months since the 1980s; as of 2013 every day more than 2.5 quintillion (2.5×10^{18}) bytes of data were created. OK, Wikipedia can sometimes overestimate the average reader's intelligence and forgets to contextualize scientific terms and ludicrously large numbers, so here is a metric you can associate with: If all the data today were bound into books (those normal sized ones and not like this manuscript you are reading just now), it would reach from the Earth to Pluto and back more than 10x, says Oracle, the undisputed software data base leader of the world, in one of its sales documents.

This is a lot of data and a lot of books for that matter. Examples of that data include web logs, RFID, sensor networks, social networks, social data (due to the social data revolution), Internet text and documents, Internet search indexing, call detail records, astronomy, atmospheric science, genomics, biogeochemical, biological, and other complex and often interdisciplinary scientific research, military surveillance, medical records, photography archives, video archives, and large-scale e-commerce.

If knowledge is power, then imagine how powerful can be the one who possesses unfettered and instant access to filtered and relevant data of unprecedented volumes. Which makes Data Analytics today's coveted Holy Grail for corporations with the desire to effectively engage with their existing and potential customer base. Data Analytics are software tools and programmes designed to take in data, complex, complicated and unstructured pieces of information and take out sophisticated analyses containing invaluable insights, not just about future trends, but also about existing habits and past behaviours.

Martin Sorrell, the head of a major advertising group, cited in 2012 the growing availability of big data analytics as one of the reasons for the continuous growth of the PR industry. As a PR man myself, I like the ring of Sorrell's remark into my ears. Finally, we have entered an era during which PR is getting the recognition it deserves from its peers in advertising. Our content-driven industry can now rule by tapping into the wealth of available data hidden dormant in servers or hovering in clouds around the world waiting patiently for their turn to be picked up by communicators who can spice up their storytelling with some compelling facts, figures and other knowledge-enhancing data.

But I fear the dominance of communications specialists, (PR's) in the marketplace will be short-lived, for the power of data deluge to transform the way marketers convey their messages is far more cunning and sinister to the health status of our long term employment prospects than the naked eye can see. Am I being a pessimist? A doomsdayer? Seeing the glass half empty? Yes! But before we get there, we have a few years of provolution ahead of us. Let's take a look into the next 10 years of the PR industry before its ultimate demise, in the shape and form known to us today.

Chapter Three

The PR industry needs to ponder about its own future and take initiatives that will help it provolve as we have already embarked on a one way journey to a world where Digital dominates.

As we try to balance on a very thin thread some would describe as the threshold between remaining competitive or simply becoming redundant, it is time to take our fate into our own hands by first defining and then shaping our future.

PR firms and practitioners need to proactively and urgently address the new emerging information consumption trends by adapting their services to the new media landscape and consumers' surfacing needs whilst adopting new techniques and practices that would help them maintain their relevance and competitiveness in the constantly changing world of the information overload age.

In the near future, writing a press release and distributing it via email to the journalists' listed in a data base while attaching a couple of high resolution pictures will simply not be enough for the media and the discerning consumers who have evolved into exclusive users of mobile smart phones and tablets sales of which have multiplied by thousands in the short while it took you to read these lines.

As we already know, in the future, print media will become obsolete or at least play second fiddle to online media. Take a look at the way advertisers allocate their marketing spend these days to understand exactly where the future of information consumption lies.

One thing is certain; the advent of new technology has so quickly changed the way media treat and people consume information that has taken most communications specialists aback finding them unprepared to deal with the real challenges posed by the revolution brought about by the propagation of smart mobile devices. It took communicators some time to be able to be in a position today to claim that they can provide reasonable strategies and tactics to simply be able to participate in the online conversations about the brands they represent. Still they have dismally failed to convince their clients of the value and expertise they can add into the overall mix by engaging with the online world.

But at least they, WE, can say that this is work in progress and blame it on the guy who dared ask the still unanswered question: "who owns digital?" Oh, I know that! "It's no one, yet, stupid!"

This time it is our chance to be ahead of the game. We must innovate and proactively seize the moment to position our industry at the forefront of the marketing mix as the communicators who truly understand where the world is heading and that we can reach there before anyone else does.

It's not just about arriving to a completely new and unknown destination but rather preparing ourselves for a journey having a clearly defined mission and carrying with us the tools we will need to accomplish our objectives.

The name of this exotic, new destination is Digital. Digital is a world where the Internet is the dominant information-sharing conduit. There are no landlines, no TV sets, no desktop computers. Instead, every person in destination Digital owns a smart, pocket-sized mobile device which can be used as a portable laptop, a phone to make voice or video calls, a HD screen to watch favourite TV programmes and other video or live footage, listen to popular songs and singers or simply be informed about the latest news, sport and weather.

This is a world where broadband width and speeds have grown exponentially together with the staggering demand for Internet services, a world where 4G networks seamlessly converge with mobile devices to provide online users with highly reliable and cost effective access to the World Wide Web in lightening speeds. It is also a brave new world where e-commerce has virtually, pun intended, replaced conventional shopping experiences—the proliferation and eventual dominance of e-commerce will at one point stagnate due to the propagation of cybercrime and this will eventually lead to an era when products will actually do the talking directly to consumers, in a similar fashion to the interaction previously facilitated through online channels. This is the beginning of the end, the point where the penny drops, figuratively, not in the vending machine.

But, the provolution of PR must continue until that penny drops.

So, back to the immediate future of the PR industry, there are no print newspapers or magazines simply because technology rendered them redundant. They only exist in cyberspace and they have evolved. They are no longer static, outdated and out of fashion bound sheets of paper regurgitating yesterday's news. Their journalists are the best-of-breed, talented few who can combine the attributes of both print and broadcast reporting offering their audiences high quality, real time text, voice and still or moving images.

In this brave new world, online information resources have also reinvented themselves and their relationship with their own audiences by offering interactive content that fuses text, images and voice to illustrate the stories published in their sites.

In this world, radio has also evolved from a voice-only medium to a dynamic forum which integrates text, dynamic video and static visuals combining the advantages offered by the airwaves in being the first to break the news with the benefits of extensive analysis and visualization provided by text and video content.

TV stations in destination Digital had little work to do in order to catch up with the times but vendors of flat TV screens had a mountain to climb to push inventory to the world's Internet-less corners and redesign their manufacturing facilities to enable them produce tablet-sized or smart phone-sized screens in order to stay in business.

Similarly, PR agencies need to stay in touch with the times in order to avoid extinction.

Agencies need to adapt by investing in upgrading their technological capabilities and in training their executives to ensure they acquire the necessary knowledge and technical know-how that would enable them maximize the use of the latest information communication technologies and keep abreast of developments.

So, would the near future PR Manager have to be an IT expert first and foremost? The answer is not really; the near future PR Manager needs to be aware of the new technologies and existing or potential capabilities and applications and use creativity and common sense to see how best it can tap into those for the benefit of agency and clients alike.

But the SUCCESSFUL PR agency of the near future will have to be equipped with the latest technologies and possess significant internal IT expertise that could potentially reside within the fictitious new role of a Creative Convergence Officer (CCO). This person will be an experienced communicator as well as an expert in the use, interoperability and convergence of diverse technologies and multiple forms of online communications. He will be able to design strategies and aggregate content from various sources and forms and know how and where to deploy them in cyberspace.

The biggest of the agencies, those which can invest in developing proprietary tools, will come up with different software versions which executives can use to create these multifunctional and multi faceted press releases of the future.

The press release of the future will have to engage with journalists and audiences in more than one way. News and information consumers are already able to move between audio, visual and print forms of communication using one device. The advent of the tablet has ushered the world into a brand new world of media and information consumption and it is becoming almost impossible to argue against the seemingly unstoppable proliferation of online media at the gravely expense of traditional print and even broadcast media.

In the not too distant future consumers will demand all different facets of the same story to be available instantly and walk the walk and talk the talk on the same screen without requiring shifting from one URL to another. Similarly, the processors of these stories, the journalists, will find it a lot more appealing if integrated content is shared with them in a single file.

A press release is drafted. Across various points, and whenever relevant, additional background information will be available to readers simply by tapping their finger on highlighted words or phrases. The background information will appear in a form of a scrolled window as opposed to a hyperlink. This way, the actual written content of a press release will be able to offer readers much more relevant information, facts, figures and other sources deemed as of 'interest and relevance' to the reader who seeks greater insight and analysis than it can actually be contained in today's conventional form.

The press release of the future will also have highlighted names of individuals relevant to the story, products, etc. By tapping on those, readers will be able to see pop ups of pictures relevant to the highlighted word without using a hyperlink. For example, in a press release about the launch of the latest iPad a simple tap on the underlined product will immediately result in a 360 degree, revolving visual (photo) selected to accompany the press release, together with its caption.

And in the same story, fingerprinting Steve Jobs (sorry Tim Cook, I started writing this before Steve's departure) who introduced the product at a media event earlier that day, would display a picture of Apple's CEO on the screen.

By clicking on Steve's picture readers would have the option to watch an edited brief version of his presentation or the full-length speech and even read his CV should they wish to learn more about him.

Or, by simply tapping on Steve's quotations in the press release, an instant digitized audio voice would simply read them out.

The press release of the future will be a totally engaging form of communicating with audiences as marketers will be able to appeal to many senses at the same time and on the same channel with zero delay in relaying and projecting the various facets of the information.

By offering this new type of interaction with the end consumer, brands and corporations, governments and NGOs will be able to convey their key messages in greater, more fulfilling detail thereby getting closer and creating a stronger emotional bond with their existing and potential customers, voters and stakeholders.

The client is calling for a press conference. OK, let's check venue availability and . . . . 'No need'. In destination Digital, information moves so fast that for a journalist accepting to spend 20 minutes to drive to a hotel and as many more to go back to the office it would amount to professional suicide. So, agencies have managed to persuade their clients that successful press conferences need to take place through Webinar technology from the comfort of the CEO's private office.

Once the text, audio and video invite has gone out to the journalists' preferred mobile device, the agency follows up and distributes unique user name and passwords to those confirming attendance in order to access the online platform.

Upon their signing in, the media may not be pointed towards the refreshments' bar by the agency's Account Executives but could instead receive a personalized on-screen greeting by a PR manager welcoming them followed by a briefing of the day's proceedings. Simultaneously, the Account Executives will be emailing the interactive and multi-media press kit to each journalist logging in to attend the press conference.

The spokesperson will deliver his speech backed up by any visual aid (slides, graphics, videos etc) required to support the dissemination of the key messages and upon conclusion the media will be invited to send their questions using the existing instant messaging technology.

The spokesperson would then respond verbally to each question until answers have been given to all media queries.

One-on-one interviews through Skype or a more advanced equivalent can then follow as scheduled. Everything controlled, recorded and documented for absolute clarity.

As a result of the congregation of all media activity online, media monitoring and evaluation of campaigns is going to be extremely accurate and transparent.

Clients will very easily be able to know what exactly their ROI has been on every single occasion and agencies will equally effortlessly be able to demonstrate the value and impact their campaign has had on their clients' bottom lines.

Every time a consumer of information interacts with a PR-generated story, either through online information resources or via mainstream digital newspaper versions, online TV or radio, special monitors will be able to capture at least some basic generic information of the person who accesses the information, ie country of residence, sex etc.

Further filtering mechanisms and additional research-led demographics analysis of each medium separately would cross reference individual touch points and be able to generate a detailed report on the average profile of people who interact with each individual story, the amount of time the interaction lasted and the ways and types—of the interaction. WOW!

So Apple would be able to know that the story about the launch of iPad 3 was read by a total of 30 million people residing in the Middle East, of whom 30% reside in Saudi Arabia, of whom 25% spent more than five minutes on the story of whom 2% did so via online radio, 5% via OKAZ newspaper's digital edition and 7% through AMEINfo.com.

Furthermore, as is already the case with social networking sites, Apple's marketers would be able to follow and participate in conversation about iPad 3 taking place on Facebook or Twitter and receive feedback from the first users of the new product that would eventually help them design a more successful iPad 4.

Similarly, the agency would be able to further segment their media targeting by better understanding the appeal certain outlets have amongst specific demographics they are targeting.

In destination Digital those will be mpeg files containing concise and succinct, yet comprehensive video and audio agency-produced tutorials about a specific upcoming event where the client's spokesman is scheduled to interact with a list of pre-determined media representatives.

The client can opt to either listen to the audio instructions in his ipod on his way to the venue or choose to watch the video on his iPad while shuffling screens containing other useful material such as pictures of the journalists he is about to meet, their recent articles as well as front cover examples of the publications they represent.

Conversely, the PR agency will also prepare similar briefing files for the media, to prep them in advance of their meeting with the client. In video and audio formats, the PR agency's team puts together a detailed but brief presentation of the key messages and questions the client would wish to touch upon during the interview. The journalist will have the option to download interactive presentations containing background information on the client.

As in any other form of communication in destination Digital, interviews must provide information consumers with all three types of content, text, video and audio. Journalists assigned to interview a company spokesman come equipped with smart cam recorders.

Information consumers can then choose from simply viewing or listening to a straightforward Q&A discussion between the journalist and the interviewee or opt to read a more lengthy, elaborate, crafty and full of flair interview story including research-based commentary as well as competitor views, illustrated with dynamic static visuals and graphics as described in the Press Release of the Future section.

And this is perhaps where the media would have the chance to differentiate its offering between free and paid for content with the lengthy version of the interview presenting a good pay-as-you-go example.

Media data bases are living documents—quite literally—residing in cyberspace but not in an excel spreadsheet in the form of a long list with strange names, dull designations and phone numbers and email addresses.

These have now evolved to eye-pleasing, colourful and compelling templates where close-up pictures of journalists are the dominant feature. By tapping on or mouse-over a picture we instantly receive a window containing full details of the individual, short bio, Facebook, Twitter and LinkedIn account details. Another click and we can view examples of articles authored by the individual.

Once individuals mentioned in the list update their LinkedIn status, our media data base automatically updates itself to reflect any changes. This would help us immediately track any changes in the status of each journalist and be able to know exactly where they can be found and contacted should they shift jobs.

The new age media will share many things in common including their ability to receive feedback from their audiences on any story they upload and instigate dialogue and debate between audiences. This is already happening of course in web sites of various media, but in destination Digital this form of interaction will acquire a whole new meaning.

Audiences would be able to choose between text, audio or video formats to post their comment on a story or reply to another comment. How powerful is that?

In response to this new world of interaction agencies could extend their services portfolio to include a 'Forum Participation' product designed to address varying client needs depending on key words or phrases used during the search stage.

Response to comments should vary from direct client message in audio, video or text to indirect agency reaction using impersonation techniques. Acting experience here would come handy.

The cynics of you out there will probably ask, 'so what' and argue that the future of the media is well known and that information consumption habits are already pointing towards a destination Digital world.

Skeptics may simply choose to dismiss these thoughts as science fiction—yet another Back to the Future type of movie—hinging on the notion of the immortality of conventional media and on people's supposed fascination with paper and ink that would never allow newspapers, magazines and books go out of fashion.

Technophobes may even challenge these thoughts (see the irony?) on the grounds that the technology mentioned in it is too complex to master or too far-fetched to take it seriously, or even, yes you guessed it, too difficult to comprehend.

This sort parenthesis endeavours to stimulate our industry in order to take the initiative that would enable it, *us*, to both confront the upcoming challenges and reap the benefits of the opportunities which would eventually present themselves to us as a result of the technological tsunami that has flooded our domain—it's time we reached for the higher grounds, the summit of our professional aspirations! Prevail first, then Perish.

Chapter Four

P R to Perish? But Sorrell says it's growing. Yes but don't forget that Sorrell's comments were made in the year 2012. Chapter 3 of this book transported you on a ten year journey till 2022 when the extinction is supposed to happen.

I am going to bring you an example from my immediate family for you to be able to start fathoming that our precious profession could be at peril, the same way as many other professions, previously considered as impervious, were made redundant due to the advent of technologies that impacted on the way people and companies communicate with each other.

Let's go back a few decades when my aunt, who recently passed away, held a job at a state-run telecommunications company as a telephonist, a job title so antiquated that even the Microsoft spellchecker on my PC doesn't recognise it. Yet, back in those days, thousands of women across Europe and the US, in the industrialised world, were working as telephonists connecting cables to little colourful sockets and casually eavesdropping into conversations of people totally strange to them.

And what about Pat the Postman? The hero of the hood, the man and in some cases, the woman who was equally revered and dreaded as he was the bearer of news, good or bad, from family, friends, the tax office or the traffic department. I haven't seen one in years, although I am reassured that they still exist, in fiction perhaps. Still, they won't be around for too long.

What happened in both cases? Technology happened, that's what. First it was the teletext and the fax machine that reduced the workload of postmen before email came for the final kill. In the case of my aunty it was her marriage to my uncle, God rest his soul too, that took her out of the misery of possessing gossip nuggets no one was interested to consume; however many of her then colleagues' careers were shattered once technological advances rendered telephone centres redundant, and with them, many aunts the world over.

As I alluded to earlier, the data my aunt was listening into during hours of eavesdropping filling her nails (I wasn't there, I am just imagining this), was relevant to nobody either because no one was interested in gossip about people they don't even know, or because my aunt had no archiving means, no information gathering mechanism and systems that would allow her to make some reasonable use of all that data at a later point in her life, either for personal fun or commercial gain.

Simply put, back then technology wasn't conducive to making chatting appealing. Which, simply put again, this isn't the case anymore. Because chatter in social media is the king of all content, or the route of all evil, depending on whose side you are with.

Today's sophisticated online content monitoring systems capture and decipher in seconds ions of real time chatter across Facebook, Twitter and other social media platforms. Companies are investing large budgets in analysing this chatter to deduce useful conclusions pertaining to perceptions people around the world have of their company and products. Technology has transformed chatter, (rapid series of short, inarticulate, speech-like sounds or written phrases) into something that can have potentially incalculable valuable; Consumer Insights! Coming directly from consumers' mouths or, to be more precise, straight from their social media accounts. Uncensored and un-vetted, impulsive and emotional thoughts of the very people marketers vie to attract their interest. Pure gold! MasterCard would call it priceless. Adidas would agree that with this knowledge, Impossible is Nothing.

I call it a day and time to get a real job.

Because, as I pointed out earlier, possession of such insightful information is manna from heaven for the marketing community of this planet, giving its privileged members a power that knows no boundaries, has no restrictions or limits as to the type of information, messaging and content they can put directly in front of their target audiences, without necessarily having to go through the traditional media channels to reach them. In any case, the vast majority of purchasing decisions are made on the points of sale, right? So, in a rather indirect way I have just proven that in the near future, middlemen such as myself, PR spin doctors, won't be required simply because consumer insights and the ability to make sense out of them will have eliminated us from the marketing chain.

Rewind back to 1994. My first year in PR. I never looked back ever since. Those were the days . . . The fax machine was always busy sending press releases, relationships with clients were much more intimate as email hadn't even been invented yet and mobile phones the size of grown man's shoe had just made their debut. The mobility I felt the minute I felt my first Erickson in my hand was liberating. The magic of being able to have a conference call with your client sitting at you favourite café in town was such a novel, albeit rather still expensive back then, feeling. What about SMS? OMG! Back then that acronym was yet unknown, CYBI?

In the early 90's, British Airways was the world's favourite airline, Marlboro was very much the cigarette of choice, the dominant mobile handset provider was Nokia (aah) and only a handful of us had heard of the word Internet. It seems now that the world back then was a crazy place. Who would have back then been able to predict that in August 2012, Curiosity would become the first unmanned vehicle to stroll on Mars—the fourth planet from the sun in our solar system and not the tantalizing chococaramel bar! Ok, maybe that wasn't that hard to predict, here is another one; who, back then, would dare utter that Greece would win the UEFA European Nations Cup in 2004? Gotcha!

In the 90's, there was only so much you could do as a marketer, an advertiser and a PR man to bring a product to the attention of the masses. It would either be through a TVC, an outdoor or print advertisement, a press release, a promotional campaign at high footfall areas, an invitation-only event, a celebrity brand ambassador or at the shelf of the supermarket or store the product was on sale at. Consumer feedback was non-existent, at least in real time. There was no real conversation between products and consumers, just a one-way monologue.

Nothing much changed till the early naughties other than Greek football fans' perception of their national team. But then, it was Armagedon personified. In the early years of social media, a Google executive said that: "Social media is like teenage sex. Everybody is talking about it but no one knows how to do it." That statement has held its truth for a while, but bears no relevance anymore. Marketers' approach to social media has matured and companies the world over have jumped on their bandwagon to develop integrated campaigns that appeal to the billions of social media users. PR, digital and other communication specialists have also become a lot more social media savvy and are capable to throw them into their mix offering clients holistic integrated communications plans to satisfy the yearn for social.

Technology is a funny thing really. In the early 90's Concorde passengers would get to New York from London in less than five hours travelling on supersonic speeds in earth's stratosphere giving those willing to part with the asking fare of 2,500 GBP a memorable view of the planet's curvy shape and more free time to hit the Big Apple's shopping malls to spend even more of their disposable income.

Banks were experimenting with ATM manufacturers the introduction of Iris technology. Surely, this was destined to revolutionize the security of our banking transactions, but decades later, consumers still fall victims of ATM scams costing banks millions of dollars each year.

In both cases, the merits of those technologies were outweighed by the hidden risks. I am not sure what held back the ATM iris technology, but as far as the Concorde was concerned, the tragic Air France accident which killed nearly 100 passengers was the turning point for the aircraft's ultimate withdrawal from operations.

No looking back though for the Internet. Despite the many hazards associated with its usage, from child pornography to bank account hacking the Internet is here to stay and with it the social media revolution.

Chapter Five

Let's make the connections with other technological developments that are happening as we speak—literally. First we have voice enabled devices, smart phones and tablets, to which one simply dictates a narrative and the device accurately captures at least 80 per cent of that content and deliver it in a print format. At the same time, we also have devices which talk back to you (Hi Suri☺) depending on the topic of conversation you select. So, we already have a basic two-way communication between semiconductors and human beings which can only get better as more advanced technologies become available.

We also have a proliferating e-commerce network of thousands of mobile-friendly web sites offering convenient shopping to millions of consumers who gradually start getting used in very personalized direct interactions between themselves and the products of their desire.

Virtual shopping baskets are filled every day with millions of items from every possible consumer category. One could argue that buying items online hides certain risks beyond the cyber threat of having your credit card details hacked. Maybe the size of the product, its colour, texture or any other variable is not exactly as it is envisaged by the online purchaser. So a trip to the mall would make more sense.

The other argument goes like this; online consumers have many more tools and insights into their disposal to scrutinize every single detail about the products they are purchasing. They cannot touch the product, no, but they have every other publicly disclosed detail about this product available in real time in front of their screen if they wish to. This is way too much more information than the one available at the consumer who does his shopping in the conventional way.

Online shoppers can enquire and get feedback on just about everything they'd like to know about a product, where it is made in, its strong and weak points compared to another product of the same category made by a different brand, if it is manufactured using unethical means, technical or nutritional characteristics, what do other people who bought the same product have to say about it and generally as much information as each individual feels is adequate to help him or her take an informed decision.

Brick and mortar shoppers the most they can rely upon is the limited knowledge of an underpaid and largely uninterested and disengaged client service clerk who would have a fraction of all available information about the same product and yet not necessarily the will to even share that with the inquisitive customers. That's why . . .

According to a January 2012 PSRAI survey conducted amongst consumers in the USA, more than half of adult mobile phone owners used their devices while they were in a store during the 2011 holiday season to seek help with purchasing decision. According to the findings of this study, 38% of cell owners used their phone to call a friend while they were in a store for advice about a purchase they were considering making. A further 24% of cell owners used their phone to look up reviews of a product online while they were in a store and 25% of adult cell owners used their phones to look up the price of a product online while they were in a store, to see if they could get a better price somewhere else.

Taken together, just over half (52%) of all adult cell owners used their phone for at least one of these three reasons over the holiday shopping season and one third (33%) used their phone specifically for online information while inside a physical store—either product reviews or pricing information.

Another survey concurs that consumers' use of smartphones to find the best deals while shopping, continues to grow in popularity. Thirty-seven per cent of PriceGrabber survey respondents plan to compare prices from their mobile phone while in brick-and-mortar stores during a recent back-to-school shopping season. When asked if they plan to do any back-to-school shopping from their mobile phone, 14 per cent of respondents said they plan to do so.

With a worldwide total of 5.9 billion (Euromonitor International April 2012) of constantly growing mobile phone subscriptions in 2011, it would be safe to bet that in the coming back-to-school season more people will consult their devices to make the right purchasing decision. And with an estimated two billion computing connected devices such as smartphones, PC's and tablets by 2016 (IDC) betting on the death of print and brick-and-mortar retailing would also be like money in bank.

It is the nature of the beast, the human beast that is, that we are inquisitive. Given the opportunity, convenience, the tools and the circumstances, we prefer to be making informed decisions based on facts, figures and hearsay that we can understand and relate to, especially when these decisions involve spending of hard earned cash or plastic dosh. The e-commerce platform holds the key to taming this natural tendency and eventually become mainstream to the brick and mortar retail alternative.

So e-commerce will continue to gain ground to the extent that one day retailing will move online completely, with the exception of Duty Free shops. The existing retail space of big brands in the segments of automobiles, consumer electronics, home appliances, furniture, fashion and other popular sectors will be transformed into 'experience' venues with bespoke ambiance and décor reflecting the values of the said brand and product. They will be atmospheric hubs appealing to users of the same brand and product or those aspiring to be. They will act as networking places promoting concepts and lifestyles for likeminded individuals suiting the specific brand and its products. It's already happening—I haven't made this up; it's called Intersect by Lexus. Call them what you may, these will be the stores of the future.

E-Commerce will eventually prevail over physical retailing in the same fashion online will deal the final death blow to print and in the same way semiconductors will make marketing so much more direct and cost effective to eventually lead to the demise of conventional marcom disciplines and the rebirth of, yes you guessed it, brick and mortar retail. Nonsense? Here is my take.

Brick and mortar retailers will fight back to regain their diminishing footfall, sadly at the expense of mainstream marketing. But before we see how they will do it, let us take a look at the existing state of their business.

Chapter Six

Global retail behemoths seem to be in crisis. Persisting recessionary forces and the proliferation of online shopping has made them less relevant than ever.

The following are extracts from an article which was published in the summer of 2011.

Growth of internet retailing continues to take sales away from store-based retailing

In addition to a varied performance among regional markets, growth rates for different channels have continued to vary substantially, with non-store retailing continuing to outperform the overall retail market. Growth rates for the non-grocery channel have been slightly higher than for the grocery channel although forecast growth rates to 2016 are likely to be similar for both.

Growth of non-store retailing is being driven primarily by the phenomenal rise of internet retailing as a disruptive force within the retail market. Vending, direct selling and homeshopping growth rates generally mirror the performance seen in store-based channels. Whilst pure play internet retailers are generally credited with much of the initial growth of internet retailing, the vast majority of new growth within the channel in 2011 has come from retailers with existing store bases. Among these retailers, Apple, Macy's and Tesco have had the most success in generating new sales over the internet.

Or, what about the following extract from a 2012 market research on footwear sales:

Approximately 19% of footwear purchases occurred online in October and online footwear purchases are up 14% year over year, the 23rd month of consecutive double digit growth! (Mastercard) The online channel is increasingly influencing footwear shopper decisions leaving many footwear brands and retailers pondering what to do on the back of the following insights:

Digital is core to the footwear purchase process: 37% of people who have researched footwear online solely rely on online resources when shopping for footwear. This means that they did not use other sources like TV, Magazines or even advice from family & friends while researching/shopping for shoes.

Footwear buyers cross-shop online before purchasing: Prior to purchasing online, footwear buyers visit an average of 2-4 competitive sites and 45% wait to purchase 2 weeks or more after starting their research.

Shoe shoppers use search throughout the shopping process: 43% of shoe shoppers use search throughout the purchase process and 39% of online footwear sales from searchers came from clicks on search ads.

Footwear shoppers search in thousands of different ways: Footwear shoppers conducted 25K+ unique query paths using category, manufacturer and retailer queries. However, we found that 18% of all query paths only contained category terms (ie shoes, boots), meaning these shoppers never searched on manufacturer or retailer terms. If footwear retailers and brands aren't appearing in search results on category queries, they are missing nearly 1 in 5 footwear shoppers! Footwear Category terms also drive online purchases. In the study, they represented almost 20% of online purchase assists and 15% of last click purchases.

*Searchers are more likely to purchase offline than non-searchers: 43%
of searchers said they ended up making a purchase in-store while only
36% of non-searchers purchased in store.*

*Mobile allows pureplays & manufacturer online stores to compete
in-store: 24% of respondents who used their mobile device to shop
for footwear, used it in the store. While shopping in-store on mobile
devices, price comparison and coupon searching were the two primary
uses for mobile devices.*

If only Erickson could just have foreseen back in the 90's that its
shoe size mobile phone would be used two decades later to actually
buy shoes.

Technology much more advanced than that Jurassic Erickson
model is rapidly reforming consumer purchasing habits, with
auctioning, and online review mobile apps driving a burgeoning
Internet retailing industry. The convenience and comfort of online
shopping is causing concerns for retailers, demonstrated by the
March 2012 bankruptcy of international electronics vendor Game,
which went into administration after it became unable to compete
with online counterparts.

On the flip side online retailers are able to monitor trends in social
media and web traffic to shape their sales and marketing strategies,
determine product demand, while cutting on labour and store
rental costs, with these savings passed on to consumers. Global
Internet retailing was worth US$399 billion in 2011;

So the signs are here and ominous for the highstreet or shopping
mall retail segment. And the reason is not just about technology.
Physical retailing is becoming obsolete also due to demographic
reasons. According to another study, whilst the 2006-2011 period
has presented major challenges for retailers, 2011-2016 is predicted
to see a return to relative stability, with the growth rate reaching
3% by 2016. However, this will be largely a result of continuing

strong growth in developing markets, particularly in Asia Pacific and Latin America. Retail sales in Japan and Western Europe, both facing rapidly ageing consumer bases, will remain relatively flat, although non-store retailing, driven by internet retailing, will continue to be a source of growth in these markets.

Even in a 2010 Euromonitor study, the signs were too strong to ignore. Some of the world's largest retailers were struggling already as the threat to store-based sales from the Internet will grow as retailers look to maximize contact with consumers, and consumers look online for value.

But, the resilient retail businesses are used to responding to consumer demand or 'pull'—it is their principal business driver. They are conditioned to adjust to the way consumers behave and they have enormous resources and budgets to enable them to do so. In short, BRICK AND MORTAR RETAILERS WILL FIGHT BACK and one way they could be doing it is through exploiting the concept of The internet of things! The internet of things, also known as the internet of everything or the internet of objects is driving many emerging trends. Defined as a self-configuring wireless network of sensors whose purpose is to interconnect all things— what does it mean in reality? More and more objects are becoming embedded with sensors and gaining the ability to communicate, suggesting the communications revolution is now extending to objects as well as people. Already smart meters and energy grids are helping to optimize energy use across networks. Looking ahead, try envisioning sensors discreetly attached to your body so you constantly are informed about how your vital functions are doing. Or pill bottles that tell you when to take your medicine; wine glasses that let you know when you have had enough to drink; sugar bowls warning you about your sugar intake. And what about presence-based advertising and payments based on locations of consumers, inventory and supply chain monitoring. Everything seems possible!

Is it?

Chapter Seven

Yes it is, if the will and desire is there, there is literally nothing we cannot do, if the right technology is deployed. And it is here where we, the commoners, the non BS or MS in Engineering or Computers, where we must pause and take some time to understand the power of technology in creating needs as opposed to what we, marketers are good at; creating dreams.

But instead of dreaming, just imagine this; you're walking in a supermarket, not a virtual one, but a brick and mortar old-fashioned supermarket with all its usual nuts and bolts. The doors open wide automatically to welcome you inside, the half smiling security guard, still standing with his two legs slightly apart and hands crossed behind his waist. The trolleys stalked in lengthy lines, you are checking a couple to decide which is the least damaged before you take on the labyrinth of aisles. A random announcement is made on the speakers about today's pasta promotion when you are entering the first aisle dedicated to household cleaning products. Everything seems familiar and in order when you can't help but noticing a small bright screen attached on a shelf. The screen is prominently placed to attract your attention in the middle of a shelf which carries a Procter & Gamble cleaning product. The screen features an appealing picture of shiny floor with the bottle of the product proudly standing in the middle. A button labelled 'press here' is also visible and as you are about to move on, you can't help but realize that the same pattern repeats itself throughout the supermarket. Screen with picture and 'press here' button always placed at the centre of each shelf. As your supermarket run today didn't include household cleaning products you didn't bother with the first few aisles but now you find yourself in between two areas selling bottled olive pickles, your daughter's favourite snack. The power of habit would previously make you reach for the more familiar brand, put it in the trolley and head off onto the next item in your shopping list. But this time, the presence of these screens, one at the pickles on your left, the other at the pickles on your right, make you hesitant. You take a moment to pause and almost inadvertently, instinctively even, your hand is pressing the 'press here' tab on the screen. A short video is playing dressed with a succinct but comprehensive narrative of the pickles. As your eyes feast on images of mouth-wateringly fresh and succulent olives picked at a farm in Southern Italy and sounds of words such as 'extra-nutrient', 'extra-virgin' etc touch your ears, you are virtually transported into a zone which is designed to change your shopping experience for ever; and with yours, those of billions of other shoppers from around the world. Real-time marketing, when is needed where is needed—a game changer for the retail industry at every level and every venue, the supermarket, the car dealership, the fashion outlet or the corner shop.

As the generic video concludes after a few short seconds, you are transfixed and confused. While you were almost certain that the picked olives your daughter loves would be in the trolley by now, you are taking more time to explore the same screen, which promotes the competitor's product. So you decide to explore a few more tabs on the screen giving you options such as 'ethical sourcing', nutritional information', 'calories count' etc. At the end of your journey to Southern Italy's olive groves, you may decide to explore your favourite brand's screen or simply get it in the trolley anyway OR, god forbid without your daughter's consent, opt for the Southern Italy olives. The same journey repeats itself throughout the supermarket. You now have so much information at your disposal at the press of a button, in visual and audio formats at the point of purchase. What would then be the need for actual marketing and PR? Right there, at the shelf, you just forgot everything and anything you knew or didn't about the product and educated yourself at the time you really needed to. Talking about bringing the concept of 'informed decision' onto a new bold level.

Let's see how could the concept apply in fashion retail. You are window shopping with your friend as you usually do on a Saturday morning. Kids at sport practice with their dad, household chores done, window browsing for a bargain is always a good way to leave behind a tiring week. You spot a brown coat at the window of M&S. As you approach closer to the window asking your friend to slow down, you find yourself looking at your reflection seemingly wearing the same coat! You are astounded but pleasantly surprised by the experience. Your friend makes a wow sound as she compliments you on how good you look in that coat! It has taken a few seconds to be convinced that you absolutely adore this coat and you haven't even had to set foot in that store, let alone wear the coat! You'd never seen before that coat in your life, nether in a TV ad, nor in a fashion magazine, yet you are now helplessly in love with it and totally incapable of resisting its appeal. What happens next is up to your wallet or the limit in the credit card of your husband who is probably blissfully unaware of your dilemma as he is spending some quality time with the kids. Spending quality time with the kids is rather not the same with spending hard earned money with the fashion retailer downtown, yet at this particular moment in time, as you grab your shopping bag containing the coveted clothing item, you decide that this was money well spent.

Impulsive purchasing is what retailers the world over crave for and marketing aids such as the one hypothetically installed at the window of that fictitious store has just proved how powerful technology is in driving purchasing decisions—impulsive ones for that matter.

Let's go back to the supermarket. Since your last visit there when you started using the screen technology to help you make the right purchase decision for you a few more things have changed.

Virtual promoters fully loaded and equipped with model looks and artificial intelligence chips are deployed at strategic locations across the store by brands paying for their services.

As you are passing by the shelf grabbing your favourite olive pickles brand, you can't help but notice that the screen you interacted with during your previous visit, looks a bit old-fashioned, out of place and obsolete compared with the new kid on the block—the good-looking, well-mannered and soft-spoken virtual promoter whose job is to make you choose the Greek olives. As you approach her, she greets you introducing herself as 'Maria from Crete, the home of the world's best olive groves.' Before you know it, you find yourself engaging with your virtual promoter in a conversation about the quality of olives from Crete, the world-renowned life span-extension attributes of Greek olive oil and the famous bitter-sweet taste of Cretan olives. This is no monologue, not a one-way narrative coming from the virtual promoter but rather a dialogue during which your questions are answered by her with accurate and highly informative content, as byte after byte of data is unloaded for your benefit in her calm, composed, confident and reassuring voice.

Some of the other products down the next aisle have adopted a more direct and aggressive POS technology; The six-pack Dove soap has inserted a 'Press Here' arrow at a prominent position on the outside cover of the packaging. You are intrigued and decide to pause and press the arrow. This is what happened next:

A small electronic circuit comprising a silicon chip, a battery, a switch, and a speaker embedded between the layers of the packaging was activated when you pressed the arrow.

The battery powers the circuit.

The speaker is just like the speaker on a cell phone, only smaller. It produces sound by vibrating the air with a small diaphragm.

An electromagnet or a small crystal generates the vibrations. The speaker is small and as a result cannot reproduce low notes because it can't move enough air to make sound at these low frequencies.

The chip is a custom integrated circuit designed and built specifically for this purpose. It contains (a) some read-only memory containing a digital form of a scripted voice-over, (b) some logic to convert the digital form of the voice over to a signal that can vibrate the speaker, and (c) some timing logic to step through all of the data in the digital voiceover from beginning to end.

The memory part of the circuit holds the data in a format similar to an mp3 file or like is what is stored on an audio CD. The timing logic is like the spring in the music box, rotating the drum so that the bumps all pass, in sequence, the music mechanism. This logic reads the data "letter by letter" (though the data is probably not stored strictly speaking as "letters" but as words.

These circuits can be made cheaply because the chip, once designed, can be mass produced, driving the cost down to pennies for each six-pack Dove packet.

And if this is just how the brick and mortar future for FMCG and fashion goods could look like, the future for automobile retail is already here.

Audi launched in 2012 Audi City, a metropolis cyberstore in London: this is where you go to buy a car as if you were shopping in a Regent Street or Saville Row boutique, with some retail bits thrown in.

At Audi City, shoppers don't peruse windows, but the digital powerwall with a Microsoft-Kinect-like interface for building the Audi of their choice in 1:1 scale and with every option represented. Audi says it is complementing its dealer network with a corporate-run presence in the city—so-called 'Customer Relationship

Managers' can be a shopper's point of contact should they wish to buy a car on the spot.

There will be at least 20 more Audi Cities opening in world hotspots by 2015. No doubt, Audi is fast tracking the transformation in the retail business of automakers.

Whether Audi is anywhere near launching any flying car models similar to those featured in the movie 'Back to the Future' remains to be seen, yet the point here is now how we will be travelling in the years to come but rather how we will be shopping.

Fast forward to 2022. Well, if the FIFA World Cup is taking place in Qatar this very year, then nothing I can add to it could be conceived as fiction.

As I said, the Arabian Peninsula State of Qatar is likely to welcome the football world to its capital Doha in 45 degrees temperature and 90 per cent humidity, unless FIFA has a change of heart as the rumour mill goes. Regardless of the final decision, Qatar was awarded the tournament on the merit of its bid. By leveraging state-of-the-art technologies, the Qataris had managed to recreate ideal weather conditions at the stadia where the footballing action will unfold. In fact, it was much easier to do this than making the authorities agree to a temporary lifting of the alcohol ban that would have precluded its consumption in areas and venues other those surrounded by the premises of luxury hotels.

A Qatar FIFA World Cup is as close to the sphere of the fictitious as is a world without conventional marketing and PR professionals.

Yet both are as close to reality as the end of this book.

Chapter Eight

So I guess this is an appropriate time to introduce you to the team of the future and Pranding's replacement, the player of the future designed to win the 2022 World cup for his Team Marketing.

1. **Crisis Management—Goalkeeper:** AS PR had to evolve and become Pranding in the built up to 2014 World Cup in order to assume the role of the playmaker, one of its spin-offs gained a first 11 position with the task to safeguard the team's defence, minimise risk of own goals and keep scoring against the team down to minimum in order to mitigate any reputational risks brought about by potentially heavy defeats.

2. **Media Planning—Right Fullback:** Together with the death of print as the main advertising conduit his influence in the team waned and his role evolved to become a more reactive, knee jerk to tactical needs, as opposed to his previous sweeper vantage point from where he used to set the tone and pace of the game.

3. **Promotion—Left Back:** He is a surprise survivor. Way too outdated and out fashioned, his presence in the first 11 is due to his long experience as opposed to his skills and talent. The coach feels that next to him, a few younger players will learn a few thngs about consistency and discipline so his place is secure for yet another world cup.

4. **Research—Centre Back:** Remains a hugely influential figure and is expected to have his best ever tournament as he is paired up next to one of the new kids on the block—Big Data. Their combined skills and outlooks will form a lethal combination for every opponent and fans expect Research to make all players more intelligent than ever before, play with their mind and outsmart the opposition.

5. **Big Data Analytics—Sweeper:** One the most promising upcoming youngsters. He started his career in the lab when his teammates were sweating out at the gym. But his vision, access to information and ability to analyse, understand and process the different variables of each opponent makes him a truly standout asset for every team. Together with Research, they will rule.

6. **Creative—Midfielder:** He maintains his relevance but his influence becomes more apparent at the POS. He had to become more straight-talking and direct so he had to abandon his flashy and flamboyant past in order to pass the ball in a more incisive fashion.

7. **Digital—Midfielder:** Since 2014 he has developed as one of the star players and both his team mates and the coach are now more confident of the value he brings to the team and know better how to extract the maximum out of him. The coach changed his position converting him from a right full back to a midfielder with offensive duties.

8. **PRranding—Central Midfielder:** Having been the most impactful player during the Brazil World Cup, he deservedly maintains a key role in the 2022 Team Marketing. Having orchestrated the team's past performances nearly to perfection and having acquired a unique all-round experience through his previous roles, he is the best man to rely upon to convey this know-how to the younger players.

9. **Social—Right Wing:** As the lines between online and offline continued to blur, he lost some of his relevance and became rather confused and disoriented. Yet, he managed to reinvent himself through different platforms and variations helping him maintain a core fan base, however disparate in nature. He is in the starting line-up because the coach still feels he has some legs before he gives someone else a chance.

10. **Marketing Innovation Chief—Playmaker:** He is the Pranding of the future. Faster than Cristiano Ronaldo, smarter than Lionel Messi. As the game continued to evolve, tech know-how and a deep understanding of data insights meant that the next generation super player for Team Marketing will have to bring his game to a whole new level. MIC, his nickname, cost me a fortune, but he is likely to prove a good ROI at Doha's futuristic stadiums during the 2022 FIFA World Cup.

11. **Shopper Marketing—**Quick and quirky, yet another addition to the team. A previous bench-warmer, he now means business from the time he turns up for practice to the time he brings the game to the opponent's end with the ruthlessness and aggression of a true predator. No questions asked, no prisoners taken. He has become indispensable and MIC has had a massive influence in helping him fulfil his full potential.

Wow! What a team . . . Sadly I won't be the one to coach them to success in 2022. As everyone else in Team Marketing, I had to provolve and decided to concentrate on writing to make a living.

But I am in the position today to reveal who the new coach is in case you were wondering.

Mr. Consumer Data Analytics.

Epilogue

Speaking at the TEDxReset Conference in Istanbul, innovation editor Thomas Frey from The Futurist predicts that over 2 billion jobs will disappear by 2030. Sectors that will be particularly hard hit include: Power, automobile transportation and education, as well as industries vulnerable to replacement by 3D Printers, e.g. manufacturing, and the next generations of robots, e.g. mining. Over time these sectors could see hundreds of millions of jobs disappearing—however at the same time these changes will create new kinds of jobs.

With 68% of all purchases unplanned, 70% of brand choices made in store, and only 5% of shoppers loyal to a particular brand within any particular category, brands and retailers today have the affordable technologies at hand that can help them treat people as active shoppers, rather than passive consumers.

The challenge for marketeers will be to evolve together with the changing landscape and enhance and diversify their skill sets to become more technologically and financially savvy.

The author

A PR man since 1994 and an ex journalist and sports writer, Georgios shares many of the vices attributed to professionals of these two industries including promoting tobacco and beverage companies and even products far more sinister that can actually kill you without warning. Guilty as charged but if he didn't do it, somebody else would anyway. But it's not all Devils' work. In PR, he has been fortunate enough to have done some truly exciting stuff such as helping the needy and creating awareness of various causes, as well as 'selling' the odd airline ticket, car, country, hotel, PC, mobile phone or a five-day Alaskan cruise. He has travelled around the world—literally—and feels fortunate to have friends in each continent. His ultimate lifetime ambition was to publish a book—which he has just achieved thanks to the advent of the Self-Publishing industry and plenty of self-belief—so now he is focusing on his next challenge—to 'sell' his book.